bp:
beginnings

bp: beginnings

bpNichol

Edited with an
Introduction & Bibliographic Notes
by Stephen Cain

BookThug · 2014

The production of this book was made possible through the generous
assistance of the Canada Council for the Arts and the Ontario Arts
Council.

Library and Archives Canada Cataloguing in Publication

Nichol, B. P., 1944—1988
[Poems. Selections]
        bp : beginnings / bpNichol ; Stephen Cain, editor.

(Department of reissue ; no. 10)
Poems.
Issued in print and electronic formats.
ISBN 978-1-77166-035-8 (pbk.)

        I. Cain, Stephen, editor of compilation   II. Title.
III. Series: Department of reissue ; no. 10

PS8527.I32A6 2014   C811'.54   C2013-908733-8
                                     C2013-908734-6

PRINTED IN CANADA

TABLE OF CONTENTS

INTRODUCTION

bp: beginnings collects bpNichol's early major poetic se-
quences – including lyric, concrete, and sound – which have
been out of print for more than 40 years. Alongside *The
Captain Poetry Poems* (1971, reissued in 2011), the texts col-
lected here now make available Nichol's long poems leading
up the publication of the first two volumes of *The Martyrol-
ogy* in 1972. Two parallel sequences to these publications,
Monotones (1971) and *Scraptures* (1965–c.1972), were even-
tually folded into *The Martryology Book(s) 7 &* (1990), while
the text of the sound poem *Dada Lama* (1968) has never
been unavailable, and can currently be found in *The Alpha-
bet Game: a bpNichol reader* (2007). The sequences collected
here represent what Stephen Voyce has recently character-
ized as "two distinct paths" in Nichol's early publications:
"a lyric mode first anthologized in Raymond Souster's
New Wave Canada: The New Explosion in Canadian Poetry
(1966), which earned Nichol early praise among Canada's
literary elite, and the minimalist 'typewriter concrete' col-
lected in *Konfessions of an Elizabethan Fan Dancer* (1967),
which aligned Nichol with an international consortium of
avant-garde writers at home and abroad" (10).

While Nichol's introductory quotation to *The Other Side
of the Room* warns of attempts at locating true beginnings
("i have forgotten how it really began (if i ever knew) so
instead i have invented a beginning, invented a start that
may have happened then"), *bp: beginnings*, nevertheless
presents Nichol's earliest publications. Only a single poem
appears in print before the *Cycles Etc.* sequence collected
here: "Translating Apollinaire," published by bill bissett in
Blew Ointment in 1964 (a poem which would later form the

basis of Nichol's *Translating Translating Apollinaire* project).
Yet despite Nichol's youth – all of the poetry collected here
was composed and published before he had turned twenty-
eight – the poems in *bp: beginnings* are in no way juvenilia,
and are only apprentice work in the sense that Nichol always
claimed he was a lifelong apprentice to language: "I used to
believe that when you turned 45 you automatically became
a master. It seemed a long time away, at the time. As I crawl
through my 30s I see that that is wrong. All of one's life in
fact one is simply in the process of learning" (*Meanwhile*
177).

Still, looking at the ten sequences collected here as a
whole, they do appear to reveal the concerns of a young
poet under the age of thirty. Recurrent themes include: the
inability to communicate, the failure of language, depression
and isolation, questions of the purpose of life and mortal-
ity, unfulfilled love, travel and exploration, and friendship.
And it is this last subject that, looking over all the sequences,
appears to dominate. Nearly every section is in some way
dedicated to friends – *The Other Side of the Room* is "for
friends"; *Beach Head* is offered up "in friendship"; *Lament* is
for d.a.levy; *KON 66 & 67* is for Jiri Valoch; *The Year of the
Frog* is for Margaret Avison; *Ruth* is for David and Ruth; and,
although *JOURNEYING & the returns* is initially dedicated
to Nichol's family, a colophon dedicates the poem to an ad-
ditional five friends, and thanks three more. While Nichol
was known for sustained and intense friendships throughout
his life, this near obsession with the question of friendship
in these early poems does seem like a youthful preoccupa-
tion that will become more muted as his career progresses
(for example, by the second book of *The Martyrology*, Nichol
has begun to use such titles as "Friends as Footnotes").

But a consideration of two key friendships does appear to be important in contextualizing some of the sequences collected here. The first is Nichol's friendship with the Canadian modernist poet Margaret Avison (1918-2007). Nichol had met Avison in 1964 while working together at the University of Toronto library, and appears to have struck up a close friendship with the poet twenty-six years his senior. At this time Avison had published her major poetry collection *Winter Sun* (1960), which had won the Governor General's award and had established her as one of the major poets of the previous generation. While Nichol would later note that Avison "was a tremendous influence, [her poetry] was an education to the ear" (*Meanwhile* 170), it is, at least on first appraisal, difficult to see the connection between these two writers. Avison's initial role appears to be that of mentor, encouraging Nichol to submit to Raymond Souster's groundbreaking *New Wave Canada* anthology (1966), which marked the first major appearance of Nichol's lyric poetry and established his reputation in that genre within Canada. She also contributed a generous letter/review of the sequence *JOURNEYING & the returns* included in the Coach House publication a year later. In return, Nichol would dedicate several poems to her, including the concrete poem "Not What the Siren Sang But What The Frag Ment" (1967), the lyric "postcard between" (collected here), and the whole of the sequence *The Year of the Frog*. In later years, Nichol would encourage Avison's more experimental side, publishing her "In Eporphyrial Harness" in *Ganglia*, and her unusual Joycean poem "sliverick" in his edited anthology of concrete poetry *The Cosmic Chef* (1970). Letters concerning her publication in *Ganglia*, as well as the comic sequence "The Innocents," would appear in *bpNichol Comics* (2002) and Nichol's essay on Avison's work, "Sketching," can be found in *Meanwhile*. The unusual friendship between the cosmopolitan modernist Avison and the proto-postmodernist Nichol was certainly significant at this time and is worth further investigation.

While Nichol's relationship with Avison was one with a mentor, his friendship with d.a.levy (1942–1968) was closer to that of a peer. Only two years older than Nichol, Levy had established himself as an agent provocateur of the Cleveland poetry scene by his early 20s. Levy developed a distinctive "dirty" concrete poetry style through his idiosyncratic mimeography, as well as through his keen interest in eastern religions, his open attitude towards psychedelics and narcotics, his "renegade" small press publications, and his love-hate relationship with the city of his birth. While Nichol's own visual work did not often resemble that of levy, Douglas Manson argues that Nichol and levy shared an interest in "do-it-yourself publishing" (197), modes of open communication within poetic communities, and "art's liberating potential" (202). Correspondence with levy also led to Nichol's contact with D.r. Wagner, a close friend of levy's who would publish Nichol's *Ballads of the Restless Are* and *Beach Head* through his Runcible Spoon Press. levy's suicide in November of 1968, prompted Nichol to compose the broadside "D.A.Dead" (1968) and the powerful *Lament*, collected here.

Moreover, it is levy's 7 Flowers Press that is responsible for Nichol's first published collection, *Cycles Etc.* (1965). Appearing in a run of 100, this chapbook has long been one of Nichol's most elusive publications, with few copies making their way to Canada. While some of the concrete poems contained in the sequence would later appear in *Konfes-*

sions of an Elizabethan Fan Dancer, and "Bouquet for Dace" would appear in both that collection and in *Still Water*, others like "Politics 2" and "Glyph #2," have not been available for half a century, and *bp: beginnings* marks the first Canadian publication of the sequence as a whole. In keeping with the spirit of that publication and Nichol's relationship to levy, the poems have been reproduced from scans of the original mimeograph publication. One can see the effect of mimeo on the aura of the poems through the texture of the ink and the almost physical impression made on the page – in some ways, *Cycles Etc.* can be viewed as a collaboration between Nichol and levy, since levy, in transcribing the concrete poems from Nichol's typewritten sheets to the mimeo, introduces errors (the opening of "Historical Implications of Turnips") and the strength (or lightness) of levy's keystrokes in retyping on the mimeo sheets can clearly be seen in "Cycle #26" and "Glyph #2."

While Nichol, in his earliest explorations of visual poetry, was calling all of his visual poetry, whether typewriter-based or stencilled, ideopomes, the sequence collected as eyes best represents his conception of the ideopome:

> My earliest visual poems I called 'ideopomes' because I had read [Ernest] Fenellosa on the Chinese written character as a medium for poetry, because I was very interested in Chinese, Japanese, Haida & Kwakiutl poetic modes, & because I saw myself as consciously working with the ideogrammatic potential of the arabic alphabet. (qtd in McElroy 63)

Originally published in Emmett Williams's comprehensive *Anthology of Concrete Poetry* (1967), this sequence marked

Nichol's first appearance in book form on the international stage, one year before his publication in Mary Ellen Solt's *Concrete Poetry: A World View* (*Concrete Poetry: Britain Canada United States*, which appeared in 1966, contained Nichol's "Blues" but was an unbound portfolio limited to fifty-six copies). In notes to the sequence published in the Williams's anthology, Nichol describes these pieces as

> tight imagistic things. intended for what they teach the eye on one looking tho some tend to be pleasing if looked at a few times. executed as a unit which has become my standard concrete composing form. seldom singly. not meant as pictures but as syllabic and sub-syllabic messages for [those] who care to listen.

For their appearance in this collection the images have been enlarged from their first publication to match the scale of similar letraset poems that Nichol published around this time, such as those found in the first issue of *Is* magazine (1967) and his later stencil work in *ABC: The Aleph Beth Book* (1971) which I believe is more in keeping with Nichol's intentions and does better justice to the sequence. Indeed, the last three images seem direct precursors to the stencil poems in *ABC* which Nichol later described as "exploring letter overlays. In a way, the thing I would most compare it to is *Nude Descending a Staircase* by Duchamp. I was interested in the play of light through the letters and what happens to the form of a letter when it overlapped with itself" (*Out-posts* 23). The three Letraset images which begin the sequence, however, appear less interested in overlay, and are closer to Nichol's conception of ideopomes in that they cluster letter forms in an ideogrammatic fashion and, like his later work in "Allegories" (from *Love: A Book of Remembrances*), suggest a narrative or metaphoric arrangement. For example, the second and third images certainly relate to perception: in the former, Nichol plays on the I/eye pun with the capital I representing the first person pronoun, and the upper case O visually resembling a human eye, while in the latter, several letter Os are arranged in circular fashion, suggesting ocular movement or eyes gazing in several directions.

JOURNEYING *& returns* (hereafter *J&R*), the lyric sequence which follows eyes in this collection, has long been overshadowed by its first material appearance as a book within a larger boxed collection (sometimes referred to as *bp*, because Nichol's first initials appear as the only text on the box's cover) that also contained a phonodisc record of Nichol's sound work, an animated flip-book, and a series of concrete poems collected in an envelope. Most critics at the time focused on the novelty of publishing such a diverse collection of materials within a boxed book-object (praising the pioneering work of Coach House Press in 1967), and neglected the more conventional poetry found in *J&R*. While this attention to the remarkable assemblage of avant-garde materials found in *J&R* is understandable, there is some evidence that Nichol himself thought of the lyric sequence as the pivot text through which the other objects could be understood. That is, one could play the sound disc while reading the lyric poems, with sound selections like "Beach at Port Dover" reflecting the imagery of many lines in *J&R*. Similarly, the concrete poem "Cold Mountain," which instructs the reader to burn while reading, echoes the fourth poem in "Part 2: Fire & Water" where the poet puts "a match to paper,/the centre darkens into an opening/the flames lick thru," while another concrete poem "pane/rain/ pain" is analogous to the fourth and fifth poems in "Part 4: Beginning . And . End." Even Nichol's choice to include photos on himself on a beach (which is the setting of many of the poems), as well as the commentary/letter of Margaret Avison on the lyrics, suggest that the sequence *J&R* is the central component of the boxed collection.

Just as the parallel concrete and sound elements of *J&R* are not included in the version of *J&R* collected here, also absent are the original material qualities of the lyric sequence. The original *J&R* is printed on grey paper stock and in various coloured inks, which make the sequence difficult to read, reflecting the content of the poem which explores "difficult" emotions as well as the imagistic play of colours in the landscape (for example, "Blues on Green" is printed with blue-green ink, while "Letters From a Rainy Season" is printed with dark blue ink). More bibliographic details of the sequence are found in the "Bibliographic Notes" of this volume.

Nevertheless, despite these absences, the sequence of *J&R* found in this text is one of Nichol's major poems, composed over three years (1963–1966), and has not been reprinted in full since its first appearance in 1967. Opening with his oft-anthologized "1335 Comox Avenue," readers are immediately presented with the themes and images that will be explored in more detail in the five sections which follow: friendship, absent lovers, seasons, elements, rituals, travel, and the relationship between the individual, the polis, and the landscape. "Part 1: Blues on Green" then finds the poet looking down on the city of Vancouver from a natural vista. But rather than feeling a sense of mastery, the speaker appears to ponder mortality and the fleeting accomplishments of urban humanity in the presence of a more ancient natural world. The second section, "Fire & Water," then moves back to an apartment space with the speaker preparing to leave on a journey, sifting through memories, and looking for a fitting way to say farewell to the city. One might expect that the next section of the poem would then explore the journey away from Vancouver, yet this component of the trip is effaced, and the third part of the poem instead picks up with a return journey from the east to Vancouver by train with this "trans-continental" element of the poem setting the groundwork for Nichol's later train poems in *Love* (1974) and *Continental Trance* (1982). *J&R* becomes increasingly modular in the fourth part, which is divided into three sections, each of which also has several additional sub-divisions. The lineation in this section is also the poem's most minimalist, and demonstrates an affinity with the work of William Carlos Williams, but also that of Robert Creeley. This fragmentation seems to suggest indecision, emotional withdrawal, and the inability to communicate which the fifth part of the poem, "Letters from a Rainy Season," attempts to alleviate. Back in an urban apartment, the speaker now appears to confront group dynamics, rather than the isolation of previous sections, eventually moving to a narrative where an abandoned seaside cottage is collectively renovated, and the poet concludes the poem somewhat idyllically, having achieved a balance between the domestic space and that of the natural world that had initially disrupted the poet's emotional equilibrium. Yet the speaker seems alone in the poem's last page, awaiting an absent friend or lover, suggesting that the anxieties of the poet have not been entirely sublimated. Certainly, as Douglas Barbour has observed, *J&R* "makes no easy promises, but neither does it offer an easy despair; rather, it allows both their places in the flow of an Heraclitean world of process articulated in its precisely modulated and always altering language" (30).

Ruth, originally published by David UU's [David W. Harris] Fleye Press, also appears to deal with the question of friends, unrequited love, and poetry, using the sea as a metaphor for imagination, change, and possibility. It is also one of Nichol's more hermetic, lyric sequences. Purposefully so, argues UU, in notes included in the second edition of the poem published under the imprint of his later Berkeley Horse editions:

> My conclusion, from viewing the drafts and from my involvement with the piece, is that Nichol was struggling with the writing of the personal [...] Nichol's solution, at this stage, was, rather than abandon his intended route to the real, to efface certain portions of its mapping, leaving a simulacrum of enigma, producing something between a language of the personal and the personal language of a schizophrenic. (UU i)

Considering this deliberate obscurity, it is perhaps not surprising that the epigraph seemed to be a red herring; astute readers might find an intertextual key to the poem through the biblical Book of Ruth. Yet, while the Book of Ruth does contain themes of conversion, seduction, loyalty, and future paternity, its central focus on the relationship between mothers and daughters-in-law, agrarian rituals, and inter-religious marriage does not seem reflected in Nichol's poem. Also surprising is the poet's assertion that poetry might function as a "real ship" on "an imaginary sea." Thinking of Marianne Moore's idea that poetry is an imaginary space where real problems might be resolved ("imaginary gardens with real toads in them"), or Nichol's own pataphysical conception of poetry as that space where one takes a "fictional staircase that you know is fiction" and climbs to an "imaginary window, and there is the real world" (*Meanwhile* 333), in the case of *Ruth,* Nichol reverses this model and postulates that poetry is the real object that goes out into the imaginary world and attempts to change that realm through its persuasive language. Of course, knowing of Nichol's later language play in *The Martyrology,* where a single letter can paragrammatically shift the direction of a given poetic line, "real ships" might not refer to poetry at all, but simply to "relationships."

Considering Nichol's relationships both with Avison and children's literature provides some clues to the context of *The Year of the Frog.* The sequence is dedicated to Avison and uses three lines from her poem "R.I.P." (first published in *Winter Sun,* 1960) as its initial epigraph. A second epigraph from Kenneth Grahame's *Wind in the Willows* (1908) follows and is taken from the chapter "Dulce Domum." Both Avison's poem, which proposes that heaven is a domestic space ("congoleum" is vinyl flooring used in kitchens), and Grahame's chapter, which can be translated as "home sweet home," suggest that the sequence might relate to childhood, the comforts of reading children's literature featuring animals, and the retrospectively idyllic associations of one's first home. Thus the sequences of images invoke Nichol's love of both classic children's literature featuring animals (Grahame's text, but also Dr. Seuss, Lewis Carroll, and L. Frank Baum's Oz series) as well as comic books such as *Pogo* or those produced by Walt Disney. Yet both epigraphs also seem to refer to the importance of alternate perceptions, or being aware of how the value of certain objects or conceptions can shift with a change of context. That is, in Avison's quotation, what is revered on earth ("diamonds") becomes mere flooring in heaven, while the Grahame passage claims that animals have "more subtle [...] physical senses" beyond smell which can indicate "summoning, warning, inciting, repelling." Thus Nichol's various images of the Frog ask us to look closer, to go beyond surface appearances; moreover, as a "character study" of the Frog in comic form, Nichol attempts to solve the problem of depicting subtle and ambiguous emotions or states of being – such as hypocrisy, longevity, or doubt – that are more complex than the more simple states of happiness or anger which are relatively easy to convey in comic form.

The two sound scores collected here, *Ballads of the Restless Are* and *Lament*, are also striking typographic visual pieces. The first, which bears a resemblance to Nichol's "Cycles" series in that it permutates the letters of a given word (or pair of words) to generate puns and new associations, signals a shift in that process whereby the poet moves not by visual association (for example, how "do" can be found within "odd") but by the ear to the phonemic potentials of letter clusters. Thus, the opening source of "roam" "ro m" and "room" generates words associated with travel, wanderlust, restlessness (to "row," all "roads" lead to "Rome," where one may have "more" experiences which one may later "rue"), or else the Romanticism of perambulation where one might encounter aspects of the natural world (the "moon," or the "moo" of lowing cattle or "rams"), or else love itself ("amore"), which might also lead to transcendental experience represented by the mantra "om." Recordings of Nichol reading this piece also contribute to the sense that this is a travel poem, with Nichol's voicing emphasizing a 2/2 beat evoking striding and striving, as well as its meditative quality through Nichol's vibratory incantation.

In contrast to the relative peace of *Ballads of the Restless Are*, Nichol's *Lament* is almost visceral in its anger. Written in response to the death of his friend d.a.levy, whose persecution by the city of Cleveland under specious charges of obscenity and corrupting the youth may have contributed to levy's depression and eventual suicide, Nichol indicts the polis itself for its own corruption and failure to acknowledge this pacifist poet who wished to liberate the people of his hometown: "you are city hall my people and look what you've done i said you are city hall my people and look what you've become i said you're your own fuzz you're your own distortions." Variations of these phrases repeat and are typographically overlayed on subsequent pages until the text itself becomes completely obscured, resembling levy's own characteristic "dirty" concrete where the distortion of letters and words through messy mimeography or photocopying begins to be more akin to abstract expressionism than writing. While the gradual return to clarity as the sequence concludes may imply a hopeful new beginning, recordings of Nichol reading this poem suggest that it is more a state of exhaustion or catharsis, rather than redemption, that is reached by the piece's closing.

Lament's "dirty" concrete aesthetic, with its invocation of decay, illegibility, and noise, is at odds with most of Nichol's well-known typewriter concrete, which is notable for its clarity, its punning play with the conventions of the typewriter keyboard, and its often regularized use of permutation. The poems collected in *Konfessions of an Elizabethan Fan Dancer* (and most of those in *Cycles Etc.*) thus exhibit the "clean" concrete poetry aesthetic, or what Gil McElroy has characterized as Nichol's attraction to "the grid." With that in mind, the sequence *KON 66 & 67* is even more anomalous within Nichol's oeuvre. Dedicated to the Czechoslovakian concrete poet Jiri Valoch (1946–), with whom Nichol would later co-edit *The Pipe: Recent Czech Concrete Poetry* (Coach House, 1973), this sequence also bears some resemblance to Valoch's own work. While Valoch would branch out to many forms of visual poetry, his mid-1960s work was almost exclusively typewriter-based, and was more expressionist in its use of the page (approaching typographic abstract expressionism in some pieces, and often not using letter forms but pure punctuation), in contrast to Nichol's lineated and punning minimalist concrete of the time. Thus with *KON 66 & 67* we can see Nichol, perhaps in response to Valoch, becoming less semantic in his language play, with some pieces completely obscuring letter-forms, and building instead concrete structures of grids, towers, and other typographic monuments. Where words are visible, most pieces suggest the poet's emotions of frustration or anger ("so much shit" or "i have forgotten the song sheet"), rather than Nichol's earlier cool intellectual play in concrete. The most semantic poem of the sequence, number nine, seems to suggest that this embrace of chaos is intentional with "order" giving off an "odder" "odour." After this point, Nichol would largely abandon typewriter concrete in favour of hand-drawn and more comic-based concrete, and would rarely return to something as "dirty" as *KON 66 & 67* where some pieces, such as number five, are almost completely illegible.

   KON 66 & 67 likely takes part of its title from the period of composition (five of the eleven pieces are dated "/66"). *Beach Head*, a sequence of lyric poems (one of four texts

which won Nichol a Governor General's award in 1970),
is also subtitled "transitions 66 & 67" suggesting, as noted
earlier, that Nichol was working freely between concrete
poetry and lyric poetry, with neither form taking dominance
in his practice. Divided into two sections, "Sea" and "Land,"
the poems in this sequence appropriately use breath lines
to explore images of water and earth, which metaphorically
become investigations of psychological states and emotional
relationships. *Beach Head*, like *J&R*, also appears to be a
sequence that exhibits Nichol's interest in the New American
Poetics of Charles Olson, Robert Duncan, and Robert
Creeley, all of whom he had read by the mid-1960s, in its
use of archetype, composition by field, proprioception,
and minimalist lineation of extreme enjambment. The four
poems that make up the "Sea" section deal with friendships
and emotional withdrawal, with persistent images of leaves,
lying, and journeys, implying a failure to connect with
others, whereas the long poem "Land" appears to depict a
conflict between male and female forces, and features the
unconventional decision to imagine the male force as aquat-
ic while the female is associated with land. Not surprisingly
for poems composed during this period, the sequence is "of-
fered up in friendship to whoever hears them," and Nichol
has noted, in a notebook entry collected in *Meanwhile,* that
the first poem in the sequence marks a shift from the flight
from the personal (in poems like *Ruth*) to the directly inter-
personal:

> 'a letter in January (for wayne clifford)' – has set the
> tone for every poem written since. the total drift of my
> poetry over the last two years (by this i mean my tradi-
> tional poetry) has been from a superficial involvement

with the self in the city or environment, to the self in the city of the self, to the self in the darker areas of the self, and now, finally, a movement outwards towards inter-relationships [...] so that the poem has become an instrument of dialogue and is seen as part of and a result of relationships or encounters with others. (24)

Just as *Beach Head* marks a shift, Barbour has argued that *The Other Side of the Room* marks a departure such that the sequence "almost seems to be Nichol's goodbye to traditional lyric poetry. The lyric 'i' in many of the poems is as often held up to question as not, and Nichol's playful approach to the individual word as potentially transformative tends to deliver the best poems from conventional lyric egotism" (34). What hasn't been given up, however, is Nichol's attention to friendship: a third of the poems are dedicated to poets such as Avison, Phyllis Webb, Victor Coleman, Wayne Clifford, the Spanish concretist Julio Campal, and the collection as a whole is "for friends." Other motifs from *J&R* and the earlier lyrics are maintained, such as interest in Chinese translation and haiku forms ("after hokusai"), trains and travel ("returning"), seasons and oceanic images ("seaquence"), and notions of urban isolation and failure, as in the opening poem, "this morning the dream will not visit me," which seems set in Montreal – unusual for a poet most often associated with Toronto and Vancouver. Although some earlier poems in *J&R* appeared to express an interest in aboriginal mythology, with *The Other Side of the Room* Nichol also explores Egyptian mythos in "title untitled" or the Norse in "varinheim." This move is in keeping with what would emerge in the early books of *The Martyrology*, where Nichol freely explores Celtic, Sumerian, and his own personal mythology of saints and comic heroes. As Barbour also observes, "[O]ne can read many of these poems [...] as sketches for *The Martyrology*, early runs at the motifs of that ever-extended poem" (36). This is demonstrated, not only in Nichol's increasing interest in multiple mythological systems, but in a new invocation of prayers and divination ("matins" or "when i am not well"), as well as poems explicitly addressing the autobiographical and his family's life in Plunkett ("circus days"), which will become the foundation for the development of *The Martyrology*.

Yet, despite these new successes, the sequence ends with a sense of failure, with the last lines of the poem "uneven song" pessimistically claiming "the rest is writ/ten the race is run//only the bad lines done." While this might point to the "bad" haiku which opens *Still Water* ("2 leaves touch//bad poems are written") published the year before, it also seems to suggest Nichol's dissatisfaction with the poetry that he has produced to this point, and perhaps his failure to unite the two strands of his published work: that of concrete/sound and that of the lyric. While I concur with those critics, and Nichol himself, who claim that with *The Martyrology* Nichol's two tendencies appear to unite, with the *trompe l'oeil* visuals of Jerry Ofo's saints and Nichol's own later concrete and paragrammatic play of letter forms at the end of Book Three being balanced with a lyric voice, I also feel that Nichol never relinquished the idea of simultaneously working in discrete visual and lyric forms. The difference is that rather than publishing them as separate units, he began to interweave the concrete and the lyric in collections like *Love*, *Zygal*, or *art facts* where the comic book concrete of the "Toth" series can be found beside such lyric meditations as "talking about strawberries all of the time" or where "love song 3" can be immediately followed by the pataphysical "probable systems 13." Rather, if we are to see these early "beginnings" as coalescing in the eventual *Martyrology*, I believe it isn't so much the lyric-versus-concrete impulse that gets resolved, but rather that the play between the personal and the semiotic begins to become less demarcated. With *The Martyrology*, Nichol seems able to sustain at one moment intensely personal and autobiographical passages, and at the next atomistic explorations of letters and morphemic slippage; similarly, at one moment he is a postmodern and post-structuralist poet, and the next he returns to a modernist quest for a monomyth. With the sequences collected in *bp: beginnings,* we see the first forays into this negative capability (of "being in uncertainties") where Nichol not only develops his concrete and lyric sides, but also attempts to merge the interpersonal with the abstract.

A NOTE ON THE TEXTS

The following sequences are ordered based on first discrete publication, rather than by date of composition or by first periodical publication. This is intended to reflect the manner in which Nichol was presenting himself to his reading public both nationally and internationally. Moreover, while Nichol very often dated, and rigorously edited his poems prior to publication, he rarely revised them after typing them out from hand-drafts. As Nichol himself comments in a closing note to *Beach Head*: "D.r. sent these back to me & said could i make any (questions) changes to these i wanted to and send them back. i couldn't. i made only one poem [different] & left it up to him. i am no longer the person i was when i wrote these." Similarly, beyond correcting typos, or changing some physical element of a book's design, Nichol did not tend to use second printings as opportunities for revising his poems. Indeed, while the one anthology of his own work assembled during his lifetime, *As Elected* (1980), contains variants or outtakes of previous published sequences, as well as unpublished material, most previously published poetry appears as it did originally. With that in mind, I have transcribed, or reproduced, the earliest discretely published version of the sequence, but have also checked this transcription against subsequent publications. Nichol's variant spellings, inconsistent capitalization, and typographic wordplay have been retained, although a few obvious typos have been corrected with the changes listed in the "Bibliographic Notes" section of this book.

Each sequence begins with an inter-title page that notes the year of publication, as well as the way in which Nichol's name appeared in that first publication as he was, at this early stage, representing his name in various ways before it became more codified as bpNichol. A facsimile of the original cover of each of the chapbooks or books follows the inter-title page. Dedications and dates of composition (which often conclude the sequences) have been retained. Further information on the original appearance of these sequences, including colophon commentary, is found in the "Bibliographic Notes."

Much of the typewriter concrete included in this collection, such as poems found in *Cycles Etc.* and *KON 66 & 67*, utilize, and are often conceptually based on, the monospace font of the typewriter, but even the more breath-based sequences such as *Beach Head* or *Ballads of the Restless Are* rely on monospace for some of their effects. As Nichol wrote in a review collected in *Meanwhile*: "The best expression of pure typewriter concerns allows you to carry over the typewriter's tremendous advantage [...] that each character occupies exactly the same space as any other character" (98). Yet, other sequences in this collection such as *J&R*, set in type by Coach House, while aware of the page and the effects of irregular lineation do not appear to rely on monospace. In trying to keep the importance of monospace, but without necessarily foregrounding the mechanism of a typewriter, this collection is set in Monospace 821, a font that, unlike Courier, does not immediately invoke the presence of a typewriter.

Special thanks to Ellie Nichol, who graciously provided permission to print all the material in this collection. Her enthusiasm for the project in general, and her generosity of spirit, kept me motivated to produce an edition of Nichol's work that would honour his memory and importance.

Thanks to Nelson Ball, the original publisher of *The Other Side of the Room*, for blessings for this reproduction. Thanks as well to Nelson for permission to reproduce Barbara Caruso's cover artwork for that publication, to Andy Phillips for permission to use his photos of Nichol, and to rob mclennan who gave the nod to reprint his reprint of *KON 66 & 67*. D.r. Wagner kindly granted permission to reproduce his cover illustrations for *Beach Head* and *Ballads of the Restless Are*, and encouraged the reprinting of these long poems originally published by his Runcible Spoon Press. Gratitude to Tony Power at the Special Collections and Rare Books, W.A.C. Bennett Library, Simon Fraser University, for providing a scan of *Cycles Etc.* Thanks to Jay MillAr, publisher of BookThug and great friend, who solicited, encouraged, and eventually produced the book.

Thanks to York University's Graduate Program in English, and Research Assistant Katie Ortolan, for excellent copy-editing, as well as the staff at the Clara Thomas Archives and Special Collections, Scott Library, York University.

Thanks to my friends Tim Conley, Victor Shea, and Andy Weaver, all of whom contributed to the development of this introduction.

Poet and artist Sharon Harris scanned and cleaned up many of the concrete poems and other hand-drawn images in this book, as well as providing conversation, encouragement, and support. I could not have assembled this book without her.

Offered in – and dedicated to – friendship.

Stephen Cain
Toronto
Winter, 2013–2014

WORKS CITED

Barbour, Douglas. *bpNichol and His Works*. Toronto: ECW, 1992.

Manson, Douglas. "Mimeograph as the Furnace of Loss: The Literary Friendship of bpNichol & d.a.levy." *d.a.levy & the mimeograph revolution*. eds. Larry Smith and Ingrid Swanberg. Huron, Ohio: Bottom Dog P, 2007. 191-204.

McElroy, Gil. *St. Art: The Visual Poetry of bpNichol*. Charlottetown: Confederation Centre Art Gallery & Museum, 2000.

Nichol, bp. *Meanwhile: The Critical Writings of bpNichol.* ed.
Roy Miki. Vancouver: Talonbooks, 2002.
---. Interview with Caroline Bayard and Jack David. *Out-
posts/Avant-postes.* Erin, Ont: Press Porcepic, 1978. 15-49.
UU, David. Afterword to *Ruth.* Hamilton, Ont: MindWare,
1993. [The Berkeley Horse 43].
Voyce, Stephen. "Foreword." *a book of variations: love-zygal-
art facts.* Toronto: Coach House Books, 2013. 9-18.

Cycles Etc.

[1965]

bpnichol

Cycles Etc.

OHIO CITY SERIES 4

BY *bpnichol*

7   FlowersPress
Cleveland Ohio | 1965
U.S. A.

<u>Cycle #25</u>

```
s   s
 l
i   a
 v
e   e
 r
s   s
```

Bouquet for Dace

y
$\tilde{e}$llow rose
ellow rose$_y$

Glyph #2

HISTORICAL IMPLICATIONS
OF TURNIPS

```
turnips are
inturps are
urnspit are
tinspur are
rustpin are
stunrip are
piturns are
nutrips are
rippuns are
punstir are
suntrip are
untrips are
spinrut are
runspit are
pitnurs are
runtsip are
puntsir are

turnsip are
tipruns are
turpsip are
spurtin are
```

Cycle # 26

```
do do do do
 odd    odd
do  odd  do
 odd  do
do do  odd
odd  do do
do do  odd
 odd  do
do  odd  do
 odd    odd
do do do do
```

Politics 2

much
   ch-ch-ch-ch-ch

        cheeps
   speech

   ch-ch-ch-ch-ch
           chum

eyes

[1967]

bp Nichol

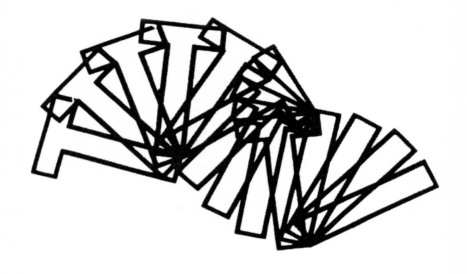

JOURNEYING & the returns

[1967]

bp Nichol

```
for
Maw & Paw
D.J., Bob & Dea
&
for 55
who started the last leg
a beginning
```

Prologue:

1335 Comox Avenue

in fall
we lose ourselves
in new rooms, gaze
from windows grown old
in that season

we choose
new beds
to love in, cover our bodies
in confusions
of all
that should be left
behind

bury our faces in each other
tasting flesh in mouth
gathering warmth
possessing each other
as a way of loving

we are too near the sea
we hear the gulls cry
cars pass
the horns of ships
and cry
to see the moss grown

throw windows open
to night   to kneel   to pray
hands on each other
pressing body into body
- some sort of liturgy

hear the sea   the bells
the sound of people passing
voices drifting up
and cold winds come
to chill our naked hearts

love is some sort of fire
come to warm us
fill our bodies
all in these motions
flowing into each other
in despair — the room —
one narrow world
that might be anywhere

Part 1:

Blues on Green

1

up on the mountain
air is
        and sky —
hot summer day
three thousand feet above sea level
looking over Vancouver
blue
   is
the colour you notice

                    "I always think within myself
                    that there is no place
                    where people do not die"
                        — Kwakiutl song

scramble up
over charred wood stumps
foot slips
then catches
in a forking branch

sit to catch my breath,
the tree
        a hundred years old
before it fell

watch the ferry,
one last puff of blue,
                    disappearing
in the strait

2

the woods
are green
            & brown trunks
letting thru the sky

soft pad of feet
on pine needles
brown & green
where the sun strikes

a hawk
circling
        eyes
the foot's slight displacement
of a leaf

            hangs

                drops

        struggles
        in the sombre green

54

3

looking out
        far over
mount rainier
& the sea

the islands
        distorted
at this distance
by the heat

            waves breaking

            faint sounds

of voices
        far below
moving over the bridge
into the city

            birds
circle round the ships
rise
    & plunge
visible only
as clouds

        sun on water,
hand on a hollowed stump,
sea calm, mountain
under my feet

Part 2:

Fire & Water

Living water should be cooked
with living fire.
                    Su T'ung Po
                    1087 AD

1

I raise the cup and take it to my lips.

this room will soon be empty,
my having been here
made no difference

I run the water from the tap
but do not fill my cup;
hold it in my hands
and taste the air

2

we lie on the bed
watching the dance the shadows do
as the candle flickers in the wind

outside my room, my room
my window shows to the world, the world
is a screen of moving shadows

"the stars are balls of fire", I was told
I had thot the rain would drown their fire
but always the reappeared.

                    lying here,
                    watching the candle flame,
                    I hold you
                    and hear the rain

3

as children
we hunched around the campfires
heat gatherers
              in the frigid air.

Looked towards the river
                    out

over
the red
       muddy
           water

                I returned to that river,
                to the cold ashes of my childhood,
                I had no fire to heat my body
                and the snow was too dirty to eat.

(once I was made of fire
held water in my hands
and drank it
felt the cooling trickle
in my flaming throat

4

(putting a match to paper,
the centre darkens into an opening
the flames lick thru)

I remember the fire we built by the sea
and the way we started it (pages
from some book) — watched
the flames turn from the paper
kindling the dry driftwood,
and the black ash,
print still visible,
drifting out to sea

5

I leave my room,
walk beside the ocean,
wind blowing in.

turning my collar up
I run along the shore
tide rushing in,
feet flicking thru
charred wood, sand, and surf

Part 3:
Ancient Maps of the Real World

prairie, lakes, trees
the whole world
falling behind

                    track
swinging away

rear platform
trans-continental

lakes, trees, rivers
dragging the eyes along

sun setting
mind breaking

drawing back
fragments
into the brain

1

eyes open on colour,
morning, fall

and the leaves, changing,
filtering light
down

thru leaves
curling, caught
in the flaming

wind
blowing from the west
cross miles of empty track

first wind to come
moving the leaves
down

past eyes,
opening,
turning

full circle,
pupils curling in
blinded by the sun

2

fingers unfolded
palms revealed

hands cupped
ready to receive

opening movements
of the sun

3

sun overhead

smoke goes
straight up

nothing moves

sun goes
from east to west

eyes & train follow

4

rolling into night
sun flame on the track,
quivering fireball
tottering
on the horizon

what myth
lies there?

eye of the dragon
coiled round the world

eye of the dragon
closing

or is it
doorway

centre of the sunflower of creation
ringed round in steam

is it fire?

flaming circle of the gods
whistle blasts mind to steam

5

eyes close
in dream
sun rises

a woman moves
hands opening
bursting the leaves
tongue roll round the sun

leaves burn
fall
thru the mind

sun falls into sea

woman
      eyes wet
breasts glistening
                  follows
swallowed in green

6

train going

mind wailing

last tunnel
last train

mind breaks
at the margin of sleep

train going down
thru valleys
leaves gone brown
falling to the sea

7

everything gone

mind shattered in the night
sun buried in the sea
woman sleeping
in another world beside him

man alone
lost in dream

train rolls on
past mountain
past night

sun comes up
gathers mind together
into heart

8

the sea
the sun

everything here

tide rolling in
ships moving out

mind in motion
eyes at rest

the continent stopped

against the west wall
called ocean

Part 4:

Beginning . And . End

I) Beginning .

1

always.

Beautiful tree
leaf

     rain

feet
leaving the grass

stains on
the carpet

bed, door, radio, open
window

wind, open
door

darkness

       says
he likes it

wants
to live there

the rest
is

history —
his

2

if to explain
then
      what?

a view
of histories
is
difficult

she hates him
and
thinks that to be it

now
other lovers

            like
            before

                        the
least possible thing
to
reach her

3

air

still
hanging

wallpaper
peeling

clothes

keep
behind him

poses
the question

i
to be him

this poem
a shadow

of him?
him?

4

early morning
rain

falling
even as

the windows
open

hands reaching
turn to

some other
voice

mountain, the
sea

   maybe
the light

          on
at

the win-
dow

   faces
to watch &

hands
to wave

possibilities
of motion

the sea

each wave
the

drops of
rain

to each
each

change
white

foam
the beach

sea

oceans
to flow to

what
to do?

see
clearly?

act
gently?

5

rain
    outside

window
open

mountains
sea

silences
to fill

no one there.

open
the door

(reverses)

6

yellow light
at
the door

blue
    windows
of early morning

lie on the bed and
wonder
when

needs
no longer
to be answered

II)   . And
           .
one of us
to go

the other
ways
      to
travel

choice
his
to leave

a place

(what if
every rock
has an etching

a face?)

80

foreign
     body

town

di-
sguised with

her
presence

brings you
down

hard

     times
travel

all of you

once
friends

ends
meet

a closed
universe

one
movement
     towards
freedom
     counterbalanced
     by

a movement

a way
back

wheat fields
some
middle point
unfound

no
map to
pinpoint
our
movements on

tensions
reduced to
nuances

and

that's when
it
really starts

III) . End


```
when
      you
come to it
            you
know

even
your clothes
hang differently

and the air
seems

        empty

from

breathing
```

Part 5:

Letters from a Rainy Season

1

the circle
is of faces
looking inwards
                towards

the centre
        of
the table

the table
at which
caught back
in the brain's shell

in the tongue's prison
till
my lips
crumble

        the
knuckles of my hands
burst forth in
raw air

the circle
turns
around me

faces
surround me
contorted as
my own

2

seated round
we hear
the sound
of feet
        across
the ceiling, the floor
of someone's room
somewhere
in this house

```
whose son, whose daughter
moves there, above us, moves
in the upper reaches
of our air

where
      do
the walls
            end
their movements
in doors

where
      do
the windows
                  frame
their world

where
      do
my own
      windows
                  move
that they appear  here
to frame
my eyes

am i
forever to see
even here
at this table
the image
of the sea?

and they
who move above us
what do
they
      see?
```

3

beyond
the eye

taken

all
that i can see

hear

broken down
for you

offered

insight
in-

side
a circling

movement

that
surrounds us

sitting

backs to
the door

the eye
turns toward

4

now the sea
brings in
its changes

the bells
sundays
ring

a strangeness
takes the heart
to windows

air   air

wherever
the sea moves
wherever

the sun
shines
or reaches

the eyes
follow
following

from the chair
seated
watching

the boats
move
ringing

the changes
the finger
traces

to bring
the strangeness
thru

5

the sun
the breast
the eye

that which
gives, that which
takes, that which

yields
is given to
and gives

that which
surrounds, that which
enfolds, that which

opens
is opened to
in opening

that which
is spoken of
and speaks

its name
upon our breath
in various guises

6

such
     care
was, taken
          to
board
     it
up
 that
even after all these years
removing the nails
was difficult

inside
the dank smell
of rot
     dead leaves
floorboards
to fall thru

          that
someone
      had
lived here
was obvious
          only
by
the planks
over the windows

```
— a whole winter
                to
fix
    the place up

it seemed
a plague,
a season
        of rains,
had struck us
left us
in the middle
of wreckage


              we
stripped it bare
(the circular
living room, the hall) where
they'd painted over
the natural wood
we scraped it clean

re-
built it — placed
ourselves there
with
what skill
we had

        the
former owner
says
        he
finds it
hard
    to believe
```

7

scrub &
the trees

the fox runs
towards the sea
from his burrow
in the hollow

a place
          by
the ocean

rain falling

where we sit
a view of
the lighthouse

each time
to venture out
seems daring

someone
we love
to wait

a reason
for returning

Vancouver — Toronto
    1963 — 1966

RUTH

[1967]

bpnichol

for david & ruth

"Why have I found grace in thine eyes,
that thou shouldest
take knowledge of me,
seeing I am a stranger"

RUTH 2:10

*

tear up our fingers

mend them
with lies

set forth
on real ships
into
an imaginary sea

the shores
vague

       lines

linking my eyes
to my heart's

        patterns

the slanting
shadows
make

moving large
above the keys

uncharted, stretching
for miles

into
an imaginary
coast

the waves carry

the torn
& broken body
of the host

end
ryme

the final bell
tolled
on a fogbound sea

eternity
a step
to be taken

over

a breath

O breathe!   salt

the lung
stings

fog
clinging
to the rung
note

***

our prayers seald
in leaky ships

cast off

"will they
return?"

"to me"

        he said

"it is so much
bad
   ryme"

(or rythm

the pace
always the same

ships sink
or are sent out again

safe in harbor
dreaming
of their faces

fingers entwine
nothingness
takes their names

held with the same care

her arms

       her legs

          her hair

june 1967

The Year of the Frog

[1967]

bpNichol

THE YeAr OF THE FROG

bp Nichol

THE YEAR of THE FROG

a study of The Frog
from SCRAPTURES: ninth
sequence

bp Nichol

GANGLIA - 1967

for
margaret avison
mistress of whimsy
who revealed the
truth of the pun
" the floor of heaven is really
diamond congoleum.
it is a rather private place "

from "Wind in the Willows"

"We others, who have long
lost the more subtle of
the physical senses, have
not even proper terms to
express an animal's in-
tercommunications with his
surroundings, living or
otherwise, and have only
the word "smell", for in-
stance, to include the
whole range of delicate
thrills which murmur in the
nose of the animal night
and day, summoning,
warning, inciting, repelling."

the
SCHIZOPHRENIA
of the
FROG

the
hypocrisy
of
the
frog

the *shadow* of
the frog

the STRENGTH

of the

frog

the
longevity
of
the
frog

the innocence of

the frog

The Frog first appeared in
SCRAPTURES: ninth sequence
which was published in
GRONK 2 available
from 73 Bernard Avenue
Toronto Canada

this character study is
published by GANGLIA,
18 Elm Avenue, Toronto,
Canada. write for a list
of other GANGLIA
PRESS publications

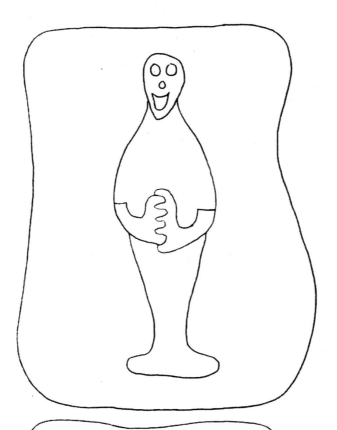

bp Nichol lives in Toronto
where he co-edits GRONK
& co-runs GANGLIA PRESS.

number 3 in GANGLIA's concrete series.

Ballads of the Restless Are

(two versions/common source)

[1968]

b p Nichol

Ballads of the Restless Are

nichol b. p.

runcible spoon

```
         roam
         ro m
         room

2)   ro ro ro
     a o
     mmm


3)   ram
     om om
     r o r o

4)   ror
     am mo
     o mr mo
```

5) rao
   om rm
   o mr o

6) rom
   amr o
   ro m o

7) rar
   omo
   mr m o o

8) rom
   amr ro
   m o o

9) ram
   om mro
   ro o

10) ror
    amo m
    mo r o

11) ram
    omo ro
    r m o

12) ror
    am mom
    ro o

13) rar
    omo r
    mo o m

14) rrm
    am mo
    o oo r

15) rao
    om mor
    r om

16) ror
    am oo
    mm o r

124

```
            roam
            ro m
            room


     2)     rrr ooo
            a o
            mmm


     3)     ram
            rm rom
            o o o


     4)     rro
            am mo
            r oo m
```

5) rar
   rm o
   o mo o m

6) rro
   am rm
   o o o m

7) rao
   rm oo
   r mo m

8) rrr
   am o m
   oo o m

9) rao
   rmo r
   oo mm

10) rro
    amo oo
    m rm

11) ram
    rm
    oor m o o

12) rro
    amo
    m r m o o

13) ram
    rm oor
    m o o

14) rrm
    am mo
    o oo r

15) rao
    rm mo
    o oo r

16) rrm
    amo o
    mo o r

KON **66** & **67** (for jiri valoch

[1968]

bpNichol

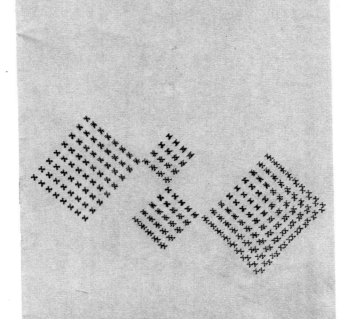

KON <u>66</u> & <u>67</u> (for jiri valoch
                              by
bpNichol

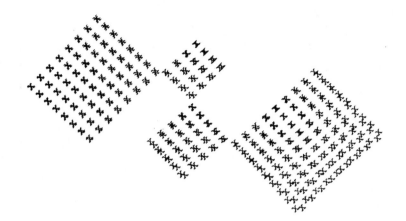

131

oder
or
der
oder
roder

16/4/66

OIDONT...JUSTDEPENDSONHOWYOULOOKATIT

16/4/66/bpn

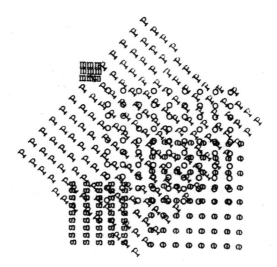

16/4/66

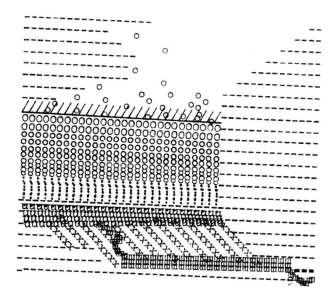

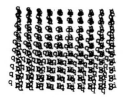

so much shit

for ml

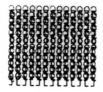

i have forgotten the song

```
i [ ] [ ] forgotten
  [ have ] [ ] [ ]
  [ the ] [ song ] [ ] sheet
  [ ] [ ] [ ] [ ]
```

23/4/66

hₕhₕhₕhₕhₕhₕhₕhₕhₕhₕhₕhₕhₕhₕhₕhₕhₕhₕhₕhₕhₕh
y.y.y.y.y.y.y.y.y.y.y.y.y.y.y.y.y.y.y.y.y

LAMENT

a sound poem

to the memory of
d.a.levy who
took his own life
november 1968

[1969]

bpNichol

LAMENT

a sound poem

---

to the memory of
d.a.levy who
took his own life
november 1968

---

bpNichol

hat you've done i said you are cit;
said you are city hall my people
ity hall my people and look what y
ple and look what you've done i sa:
what you've become i said you are
e i said you are city hall my peop;
re city hall my people and look wh
my people and look what youve beco:
ook what you've done i said you ar
ve become i said you are city hall
d you are city hall my people and
y hall my people and look what you
e and look what you've become i sa:
hat you've done i said you are cit;
come i said you're your own fuzz n
d you're your own distortions and
ty hall my people and look what yo
e and look what youve become i sai
ok what youve done i said you are
become i said you are city hall my
ou are city hall my people and loo
ty hall my people and look what yo
le and look what youve become i sa
what youve done 9 i said you are
ecome i said you're your own gover;
're your own people you gotta make

, are city hall my people and look w
people and look what youve become
k what you've done i said you are
ome i said you are city hall my pe
u are city hall my people and look
l my people and look what youve do
k what you've become 8 i said you
u've done i said you are city hall
d you are city hall my people and 1
y hall my people and look what you
le and look what you've done i sai
t youve become i said you are 1 cit
e i said you are city hall my peop
are city hall my people and look w
l my people and look what you've be
le and look what you've done i sai
t you've become i said 6 you are ci
e i said you are city hall my peopl
you are city hall my people and lo
ll my people and look what you've
b and look what youve done i said y
hat youve become i said you are ci
e i said you are city hall my peop
u are city hall my people and look
l my people and look what youve b
you can't shuck it now i said you
ehow i said you are city hall my p

i said you are city hall my peop
ity hall my people and look what y
pple and look what youve done i sai
hat youve become i said you are ci
e i said you are city hall my peop
are city hall my people and look w
y people and look what youve become
ook what youve done i said you are
uve become i said you are city hal
y you are city hall my people and 1
hall my people and look what youve
e and look what youve done look wh
ne i said look what youve become i
k what youve become i said you are
done i said youre your own dister
are city hall my people and look w
ne i said look what youve become i
youve become i said look what youv
aid look what youve done i said lo
ve done i said look what youve bec
k what youve become i said look wh
me i said look what youve done i s
t youve done i said look what youv
id look what youve become i said 1
become i said look what youve don
k what youve done i said look what

ⁿℲ what you've done i said you are /hat you've done i said you are cit
ⁱome i said you are city hall my pe,hstiⱨoⱨⱨⱨoaⱨoneitysⱨidlyoⱨ preⱨdit
ⁱ are city hall my people and look, iⱨⱨiⱨaⱨⱨuⱨyⱨpeeⱨⱨy ⱨⱨⱨlⱨoⱨkpⱨbⱨleⱨ
ⁱl my people and look what youve do,ⱨⱨⱨ ⱨⱨⱨllⱨyⱨkpⱨoⱨleyⱨndvⱨoⱨⱨnⱨⱨⱨsⱨⱨ
l look what youve become i said you.ⱨⱨⱨterⱨdulⱨoⱨbⱨⱨoⱨⱨyduⱨⱨⱨddⱨnⱨ irⱨaⱨ
wa done i said you are city hall m.whⱨtsⱨⱨu'youbecomeityshⱨdlyoⱨⱨ propⱨ
id you are city hall my peopl2 and.ⱨeicⱨⱨyⱨhⱨⱨⱨ myepeⱨtⱨeⱨⱨⱨ ⱨⱨcⱨeeⱨⱨ
lity hall my people and look what y.ⱨⱨ pⱨtplⱨⱨlⱨdⱨyopⱨoⱨhetⱨⱨdulⱨoⱨⱨⱨⱨ
iple and look what youve done i ssi.ⱨⱨkpⱨoⱨleyⱨndvⱨoⱨⱨnⱨⱨⱨtsⱨⱨuⱨgoⱨeⱨⱨ
t youve become i said you are city.ⱨokⱨⱨⱨⱨⱨyⱨuⱨⱨⱨddⱨnⱨ ⱨrⱨaⱨdtyoⱨⱨⱨⱨ
ie i said you are city hall my peop.ⱨeyⱨⱨⱨomⱨ tⱨsⱨⱨⱨⱨⱨⱨⱨuⱨyrⱨecⱨⱨⱨy ⱨⱨⱨl
ve become i said look what youve d.ⱨ ⱨⱨⱨlⱨⱨⱨ pⱨtplⱨⱨⱨⱨⱨmⱨopⱨoⱨⱨⱨⱨtⱨⱨⱨuⱨ
d 5 look what youve done i said lo.ⱨ ⱨⱨⱨllⱨyⱨkpⱨⱨⱨⱨeyⱨndvⱨoⱨⱨoⱨhⱨtiyⱨuⱨ
fuzz my people and look what youv.ⱨⱨⱨndⱨⱨⱨdⱨⱨ ⱨⱨnⱨ ⱨⱨuⱨⱨd yⱨⱨomⱨⱨicⱨⱨⱨ
look what youve become i said you.hⱨteyⱨuⱨⱨⱨddⱨnⱨ'ⱨⱨⱨⱨⱨdⱨryoⱨnⱨfⱨzⱨⱨⱨ
ve done look what youve become i s.ⱨomⱨuⱨrⱨⱨⱨdⱨyoⱨⱨnⱨdⱨoⱨⱨoⱨⱨⱨnⱨuⱨⱨⱨⱨⱨ
ve become i said look what youve d.ⱨyyⱨⱨlⱨⱨⱨyopⱨⱨpⱨn ⱨⱨⱨtⱨⱨⱨⱨⱨⱨⱨⱨⱨnⱨoⱨ
k what youve done i said look what ty.hⱨllomⱨ ⱨⱨⱨⱨlyoⱨⱨd ⱨⱨoⱨⱨⱨⱨⱨⱨtsⱨⱨⱨ
e i said look what youve become i .ⱨⱨⱨⱨⱨⱨⱨlogⱨⱨuⱨⱨⱨⱨoⱨoⱨteⱨⱨⱨⱨoⱨⱨⱨⱨⱨⱨⱨⱨ
t youve become i said look what yo.ⱨkⱨⱨⱨtⱨyoⱨⱨⱨ ⱨonⱨⱨⱨⱨeⱨeⱨⱨⱨyyⱨⱨⱨⱨⱨⱨⱨ
aid look what youve done i said lo.ⱨⱨⱨⱨomⱨ ⱨⱨⱨⱨⱨⱨⱨⱨⱨⱨuⱨyrⱨecⱨⱨⱨy ⱨⱨⱨllⱨⱨⱨ
va done i said look what youve bec.ⱨⱨ ⱨⱨⱨlcⱨⱨyphⱨⱨlⱨⱨⱨⱨⱨⱨⱨⱨpⱨⱨ whatlⱨoⱨ
k what youve become i said look wh.ⱨy hⱨⱨllⱨyⱨkpⱨⱨⱨⱨeyⱨⱨdⱨlbeⱨoⱨⱨⱨi yⱨ
me i said look what youve done i s.ⱨwhⱨnⱨyⱨⱨⱨ ⱨhⱨⱨ yoⱨⱨⱨⱨⱨⱨⱨⱨⱨ ⱨrⱨⱨⱨ
t youve done i said look what youve.ⱨhⱨt yoⱨⱨⱨⱨdⱨnⱨ'ⱨⱨiyⱨⱨⱨdoⱨⱨⱨgⱨrⱨrⱨ
ℲS look what youve become i said lo.ⱨⱨomⱨoⱨrⱨoⱨⱨd yoⱨⱨⱨe yourgoⱨⱨⱨgⱨⱨⱨⱨⱨ
become i said look what youve done.ⱨⱨⱨⱨⱨⱨⱨⱨⱨⱨⱨoⱨⱨⱨⱨⱨⱨⱨⱨ ⱨⱨⱨⱨⱨⱨⱨⱨⱨⱨⱨⱨⱨ

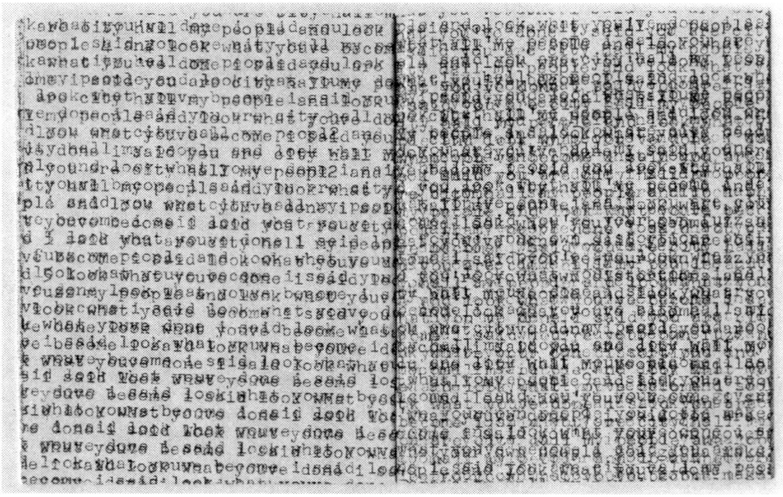

are city hall my people and look

ity hall my people and look what y
ple and look what youve done i sai
hat youve become i said you are ci
e i said you are city hall my peop
are city hall my people and look w
people and look what youve become
ook what youve done i said you are
uve become i said you are city hal
you are city hall my people and l
hall my people and look what youve
e and look what youve done look wh
ne i said look what youve become i
k what youve become i said you are
done i said youre your own distor
are city hall my people and look w
id look what youve done and look w
ne i said look what youve become i
youve become i said look what youv
aid look what youve done i said lo
ve done i said look what youve bec
k what youve become i said look wh
me i said look what youve done i s
t youve done i said look what youv
id look what youve become i said l
become i said look what youve don
k what youve done i said look what
lookwhat youve become i

k what you've done i said you are
ome i said you are city hall my p
are city hall my people and look
l my people and look what youve d
look what youve become i said yo
ve done i said you are city hall
d you are city hall my peopl2 and
ity hall my people and look what
ple and look what youve done i sa
t youve become i said you are cit
e i said you are city hall my peo
ve become i said look what youve
d 5 look what youve done i said lo
fuzz my people and look what youv
look what youve become i said you
ve done look what youve become i s
ve become i said look what youve d
k what youve done i said look what
e i said look what youve become i
t youve become i said look what yo
aid look what youve done i said lo
ve done i said look what youve bec
k what youve become i said look wh
me i said look what youve done i s
t youve done i said look what youv
d look what youve become i said lo
become i said look what

hat you've done i said you are cit
said you are city hall my people
ity hall my people and look what y
ple and look what you've done i sa
what you've become i said you are
e i said you are city hall my peop
re city hall my people and look wh
my people and look what youve beco
ook what you've done i said you ar
ve become i said you are city hall
d you are city hall my people and
y hall my people and look what you
e and look what youve become i sa
hat you've done i said you are cit
come i said you're your own fuzz n
d you're your own distortions and
ty hall my people and look what you
e and look what youve become i said
ok what youve done i said you are
become i said you are city hall my
ou are city hall my people and look
y hall my people and look what you
e and look what youve become i sa
what youve done 9 i said you are
come i said you're your own govern
re your own people you gotta makei
ople and look what youve done i

are city hall my people and look
people and look what youve become
k what you've done i said you are
ome i said you are city hall my pe
u are city hall my people and look
1 my people and look what youve do
k what you've become 8 i said you
u've done i said you are city hall
d you are city hall my people and
y hall my people and look what you
ple and look what you've done i sa
t youve become i said you are 1 ci
e i said you are city hall my peop
are city hall my people and look
1 my people and look what you've b
ple and look what you've done i sa
t you've become i said 6 you are c
e i said you are city hall my peop
you are city hall my people and 1
all my people and look what you've
e and look what youve done i said
what youve become i said you are c
ne i said you are city hall my peo
ou are city hall my people and loo
11 my people and look what youve
d you can't shuck it now i said yo

this poem was first per-
formed as part of a rea-
ding in conjunction with
the opening of an exhibi-
tion of concrete poetry
at the UBC gallery of
fine arts.
                april 1969

published may 3 1969
by GANGLIA PRESS c/o
thevillagebookstore
29 gerrard west toronto
            C A N A D A

Beach Head

transitions **66** & **67**

[1970]

b p Nichol

SEA

a letter in january

                    to wayne & julie clifford

*

having risen from the bath
old images return
                    sea
moving into me

                    only the echoes left

what moves now are ghosts
(hosts of the old forms)

as ships moved westward where
a continent crumbled

having struggled this long

what the eye sees leaves no return
from that one journey that accords
a turning to your world
(a shift of forces)

**

this night the sea moves into me

dark street

no way of sailing over it
& so i must move thru it alone
                                nameless
& walk beyond my lies

but the words are on me   hang heavy
& the voice cries to be heard

inside me all inside me

dark world

***

we can say the myths end
return full circle &
the actual untangles its confusions

the world is given its history

his story never changes

some journey is done
& the ear gathers the words near
to measure what one has won

SEQUENCE

morning:

morning spreads
its soft fat fingers
over our faces
pokes them
into our eyes
sur-
prising us awake
with soft punches

afternoon:

a-
way.   a way
of looking at things)

keep moving, shifting
perspectives

(never see into it
never get close

evening:

being becomes
counting the ways
you've trapped yourself
or(i
should say) can
come to that. be
careful
of lies like "i
love you"   ties
that bind you
when
you really can't

RELATIONSHIPS

for Dave Phillips

the space
between

a leaf
fills

all
possible motions

touch
both sides

leave us
here

THE FUGITIVE

for issac

1

the law is
inside me
bids me bide
my time
& tide
is the daily
rising
of emotions — "who
are they? what
do they
want? when
will   they
fail   me?"

2

"now far
to go to
the border?"

sat tall in
the saddle

now they
hunt him down

stoop-shouldered
half-a-
day's ride from
the other side

3

the problem at
this point

how to
face yourself, the sun
inside

your eyes
burning

4

"locks open
very
easily" the key is
in the statement
she had said
he knew

5

to get
inside the border
is to be
inside
a matter of
living
to get out

LAND

as I
is eyes

as
I am now
able
to see
clearly
the way
before me

as
I am now
whole
and able to be
here

so
I would give you
vowels, vows,
that my nouns
make, breaks
in the silences
my mind
had made
as it moved
(not thru
the I
for
the eye
was closed) in
the past —

tense (as
I was
then in
my speech
even) uneven
the rhythm
broken by
the to & fro
motion of
the eye
lid

as I hid
the light
from myself
saying
others
had done so

so my eyes
now
open
letting
the light
in, as
my mouth
opens
letting
my tongue
order
the verbs
the light

has moved
to action

as impulse as
now
my blood
races, the heat
the light
brings bringing
the words
forth in
such heat
the heart
flows
with them

as
I do
now
flow
the eye
open, one
continuous
circling, light
into light
into light

1

what visions i have come
not with the night
not with the chaos but
the memory of chaos
as now
    at journeys end
i have emerged from chaos
into the infinite order
of light, my eyes
open
to the suns light
the moon reflected
as cold surfaces will
when i walked in chaos
when
    the chaos was in me
and ruled me

what visions i had then
were of the chaos
seen as
        an infinite jumble
of shadow & dark thots
the head remembers
long after the dark is gone,
long after the light has come
penetrating
the farthest reaches
of the soul

& the soul remembers
in speech (the scarred
syllables) & the speech
flows
& cleanses

2

what has begun in darkness
remains there
       tho
we would have it here (one
i had loved then
as love was possible
when
      it was myself I hid from
in her — as she was mirrors
i saw myself in — as
we are mirrors for each other,
the dark turning of
our souls, caught
as the moon is
servant of
the sun) beside us
as it was
then (as she was
beside me
& the darkness
in her — as she became
the darkness
inside me — a desperate
reaching for the moon in
the darker pool within
         & cannot be
again

```
        the sun fell


                        away
        as the light fell,
        as I fell
        into the darkness
        knowing
        the sun
        would fall
                    thru
        into the light
        again

        knowing
        the light
        would fall (as she knew,
        she said, that I
        would fall
        from her (as she fell
        into the darkness, turning
        & turning) my words
        a turning
        of my dark side
        from the sun's
        light) away

        into the dark
        the light threw
```

```
up
    into my eyes,
the words
upon my face
in the moon's light

speaking
from our eyes
in the darkness,
the outer edges
of our skin
touching

the grace
of touch
gone, a
stumbling
motion
we spoke of
(then) as love
```

under the sea
we were poor fish creatures
our desperate voices
crying to each other
in the darkness

tho she was land and
i hungered for her
my floundering drove me down
further and further from the light
till only the dark was there
(the silver bubbles of her breath) and
she was not there
and
     i could not reach her

4

```
turning from darkness
the sun came, as
turning
a voice came
back to me
I did not know, as
she came
&
I did not know her
tho I had lain by her
in the darkness (the voice
my voice, the words
twisted
& strange
as she was
made strange
by my mind's
darkness) &
the dark
receded
till only
the far edges
remained
& my eyes
were opened
in the sun's
light
```

5

a calming.

our breathing
changes.

                measuring
our footfalls
we mark our entry
into the light.

                    tho
the memory
of
      the dark
lingers
            we
place it
beyond ourselves.

the light
enters is
all around us (and
she is apart
                from me

cannot be
near me
again)

we move

        separately

the knowledge
of
each limb
assures

always
the memory of
the darkness
clings

a darker opening in
the heart of things

The Other Side of the Room

poems 1966—69

[1971]

bpNichol

OF THE ROOM

if you want to start somewhere you should start at
the beginning tho i suppose too often i have begun
in the middle of things or ended there so that the
borders finally become blurred. now it is impos-
sible. i have forgotten how it really began (if i
ever knew) so instead i have invented a beginning,
invented a start that may have happened then (if
it hasn't happened now) and what does it really
matter? it doesn't matter. the life i lived then
was a lie as is the beginning (if it is a lie) and
i have chosen to begin over again. so that this
beginning, not being the same, seems first of all
in importance.
        if you want to start somewhere be-
gin here or begin in the middle. if you want to
start start somewhere.
        it's been so many years now
i've forgotten what really happened but i suppose
that that is least important. what i do remember
i've recorded here and what i don't remember i've
recorded here. i had to know.

(unfinished novel — 1967)

for friends

***

this morning the dream will not visit me
awakened to the traffic on cedar avenue
i have driven over the bridges
and am no longer there

the hall is wide
wider than the river that flows &
the sword that is offered
                              i cannot take

              what holds me now?

it is surely death head caught in the poem
surely my own life
lost beneath the speeding cars on cote des neiges

remember a time
the lines flowed thru me
simply to be born

                    stare at my watch
losing myself
                my mind

all that's encompassed ends

all that was song & meaning lost

sound of machinery tossed back from
cold high walls

                        for dave & denise

***

of stupidity well
maybe your eyes work backwards
and Baal's alphabetic spectre
plagues your sleep
flecking the skin with dreams of inconstancy
so that the skin (diseased)
takes on a life of its own
separate
          from the mind

there was a time

i remember dreaming screwing this whore
in a back street
bedroom
          farce

Fred Astaire as
the bell-ringer
carting the plague victims
home

          and me (oblivious)
losing my sense of time
in a faceless ending

ah constancy

i have not heard your breathing
a long time

the bell-ringer set himself on fire to cleanse his
soul

i set fire to the back street
and nearly burned the town down

so someone said

why don't you just
turn around?

186

***

                a thin thing
in all things

a thin   surface
below the   face of   everything

every thin thing which delights us
lies below the surface of
another thing

<u>the end of et cetera</u>

it's hard to remain tragic when you're not

some things end

some people have lovers
some have friends

strange to discover you're not really where you thot

you sit there
with a sudden
different face

think a lot

a strange place

<u>after hokusai</u>

the old man holds
the sea on a
string. how can he
bring it in &
keep from drowning?

junctions

for stan kog dennis wayne & juli

they play
the finger game

criss-cross their palms
as mine are
with markings of their lives

bring each other closer
with their touching

touch heart
              stones
trembling in
their pockets

fingers meeting nails
where skin bends

bending into love
eyes open
all openings speech flows from
some tongue where
beyond words
all birds
fly

**

if i am beyond words
i am behind my tongue
throat clogged with phlegm

&

speechless lest my words harm
language seems young
compared to noise

foaming in my lung
a bird dies
as all words must

&

there is no junction
where i can contend
inside such lies

**

stone bend
& end
such questings
as plague me

in a time when on words talk
& clocks are tricked by useless turnings
what questionings the birds warn of
revolve on openings

i am left open
& words come & go beyond my reckoning

a junction of seasons
where reasonings melt

& snow

9pm blues

lie in the dark
room of
the head

        wait
for someone
to lift the dread
           from me

who comes?

there is
no breathing but
        my own
           alone by
           the radio

dance head

be done and
be fled

varinheim

word
you are world again
& i am finding you slowly

my love (who she is)
a small woman
with small hands

walks
& is words
my tongue can't speak

triplets of praise
knotted in
my head

i move slowly
with too much awkwardness
to afford to lie

you

woman

i was afraid
to call
        your name

felt the lies
move in my eyes
against you

lost my way
by
refusing you

find
even the simplest speech
ugly

because i cannot
speak my heart
truthfully

<u>unfinished song</u>

woke up in the morning
nothing in my head

woke up this morning
wishing i was dead

there was no sun in the east
& all the stars had fled

change (changing)

rolling back
inside my eyes
the trees
        were never more themselves

i've dreamt too often to remain unaware

travelled the same road to meet her a dozen times

now she invades my last refuge

i fling poems at her
& make for the other side

---

                        far edge
                                far region
                        no reckoning
                                to be done

                        i said "come back again"
                        as tho i'd erased

the bad times:

            :sunset

            the house sinks
            on the water

            i shoot my mind full of darkness

            "come back again"

            falling &
            unaware

            that was
            later

"first to remind…"

try speaking now

now
    please

trying speaking now

                        i thot she'd
                        never shut-up

"just keep walking" i said
"it'll make sense later if you
just keep moving"

the trees were
never more themselves

        never less ourselves

        never the less for
        trying

"you keep changing" she said
"i can't   get you
 in   focus"

      memories

          of a distant
          time

          dark room

          bodies

          locking

          into
          position

.

no room
a voice says

no voice but
my own

my tongue inside
my head where
my eyes turn

***

if there is one i've sought
who is she
        who is not
the ones i've found

never in my life
                i've known peace

seldom can i hear   see
clearly

now i know less than when i started
of what little there is to know

please grant me peace
                    who are
                        who hear

and know

***

out of the middle the ends are taken
broken & bleeding
                    the head in the dream
fell from its body   the gun
tore a hole thru   her belly

waking
tongue breaking thru into a scream
the lines covered over the words i'd said
love was a door that did not open
into the mind
                    & the lines from
my palm to my thumb
showed the life i was to lead

taking her hand   the dream so old
it could not hold the violence in
breaking up   out of the lost corners of
the brain   i came to the lies my eyes could see
staring into the darkness

<u>seaquence</u>

for phyllis webb

a new beginning
begging
        for an ending

but nothing

no string
to tie it up
neatly

the fisherman weaves his nets
but cannot spell

the sea
        finds its way thru
into   wells   the farmer digs
praying for rain

major mover is a tide that pulls   steady
till the force is   tidal

and the farmer casts his runes in despair
fleeing into waves struggle in nets or

carried to well's bottom

to stare up disconsolately
into the face   his seed   begets

**

the sea
a mirror
     the heart skips upon
when thrown carelessly

as words are
         often
in a poem

      or
as a friend said
"'love' words are"

cheap
    i said
casting my heart into the sea

all things return to some shore

one searches all one's life
to fill the core's
emptiness

       waiting

anywhere the tide comes
in

   into

come into me

**

poems

friends give
to friends

        gestures

somehow
to cross
the real world

          of fantasy

into a real world without words

as in the poem
a syllable's discarded
to reveal a real breast

             "the rest
             is
             history"

in a minor key

no music for major mover
that is not his
        hers

eventually

<u>hi stories</u>

for vic & sarah

light in the windows of third storey rooms

the simplest things   become charged
with memory

                    out of season
leaves fall
                  cracked & dry   the sky
a clear windy blue
                      deep & dark
                              as history

history?

his story is an old one

to some of us
standing in the narrow corridors of our homes
familiar

            familiar as hands are
that've known a touch
a long time

                a longing time

only the rub of cloth against a dry thigh to contend with
we are charged with keeping a lie together

the fingers are futile
                        & too far apart
to work properly

what light glows
does not grow

                but is turned off

<u>a week of quiet</u>

for wayne & juli

this night (late January)
i watch the rain fall
from the front porch of
                    my home

cold   there is no magic
to reply with

                    what magic
is there?

            now i have
mementos   things
i speak of with
my fingers   to give

mementos
        worn

around
        the neck

                heavy as
the small dead fingers of
my childhood

**

i place the dead
against the dead

some source of
statistics

their numbers
increase

the number of things done
does not increase

only a movement
towards the interior

strangely
when the moon is dark

**

light from
the street lamp

no moon tho
the rain
stop

     there is
no trickery in
the shadows
i have not
seen   before

one speaks of mementos &
the hands seem dead

one speaks with ones hands &
the fingers fall

                    feathers & lead

***

for julio campal
who died april 19, 1968

be near
been here
too long
to long

long to
been near
to hear
belong

<u>peace</u>

for chris baumann
(two days after the massacre)

the tree idle

even the wind
finds movement
an effort

such still days are only heartbreak

give me
the wind
          always
a new song

a way to find one
when everything's gone wrong

& trees
ever moving
to walk under

<u>for ellie</u>

the poem spreads outward
the softer edges of language opening
"like a flower"
                a friend said
                            like a flower

                                        balance

holding the poem on   the tip of
my tongue
            the tongue is
heavy

        heavy as rain the poems fall

        flowers & rain where language flows

(green buds on
                the tongue

**

on the petal's edge

                        oceanflower
                        sunflower

                    to

let one's self go
                    down
flow   into
            the round

                        voices   (a song for
the sun's flowering
                    now
at the tips of   darkness

                                        (your presence flowing in

clover   onion   honey

strange spells my voice can sing

**

into the flower
making the body flower   the body
                                flow

                                        lower
                        in the mind

                        (where the blind walk   past me

sea-city behind me   lost
in the past passage of
                        a bad poem

de
cember   that close to
some hope

        the blind rattling against
the pane

poinsetta to be reached

each petal allowed to open

flowering

            each to each

<u>the other side of the room</u>

lovers   the skin is
a way of touching

                    hello

always the glass
between you &
what goes past

returning

to a
far country

a strange
train

you were
standing in
the stations

i said i
was sorry but
i had to
go

    you
turned away

the window is
frosted over

i couldn't hear you breathing

lost in
the steam and
wheels

the windows were
thick with
your breath

i couldn't see you

all along the   way

**

```
wire fence
tight against
the track

wood slats
grayed and split by
sun

     rain
no longer
here

a winter world
                words
cannot
        stand against

i stretched my fingers over the window
trying to see you thru all that frost

i found myself in a gray country
without friends

i did not know who you were
& could not reach my lips
to tell you


          whistling

long and
drawn out

          winter night

Blue
River

"in the heart"
```

**

narrow slit for
the eyes

snow blindness

sun dogs
holding sway

two hearts
the veins run from

too much blood for
the head to
handle

giving up

under the crunch of   tracks
made heavy by
clothing

so much clothing
against the cold

so much cold against
the windowpane

the head lies

growing

**

to finally admit to love

the engine screams in
the dark wood

too far
to go

the mountains were high and
impossible to
scale

the sea had
edges

where things dwelt

eager to
kill

**

```
part of the terror was
finding the edges
weren't there

sailing over
into
      a round world

a whole continent to span

nothing is encompassed but
the mind

held in against
the world beyond
```

**

you have moved into the poem
as love does

                    or fear

it is a cold window
holds the terror free

a dark room

a train

too many heads
leaned against
the moving
scenery

<u>winter song</u>

the trees move with such grace
i would there were leaves
to fill the spaces
between them   but

it is winter

it snows

may the season
teach us her wisdom
before she goes

<u>circle</u>

it is afternoon.
the sun shines.
the moon will rise
(eventually)
                over tea
she tells me.

<u>old years poem</u>

for visvaldis

i looked into my life as into a deep well

my sister & my mother rose before me

the unimaginable hell of
my early years
                    forgotten
behind the laughter
the fears
              provoked

yoked & chained
i fell
into my passions

screaming my hate and love across the years
my tears will not flow thru

to have loved you & lost
all hope of pleasing
                    the way i would have
could i have reached you

                         the skin would not admit
of being
bound by the past struggle to contain
the mounting pain

seeing my mother strain against
the years' anguish

beauty to languish
in the dull routine
of growing older

                    told her again & again
my promise to free her
from the traps of time

                         & now she ages

& i rage
within   the knowledge of
my failure

                 sure i grow old as she does
crushed by the weight of a sadness we both contain

no way of ending these words
knowing the hurt is not heard
nor ever can be

title untitled

called forth the gods
(the old ones)

               on my knees before them

as one who travelled far from his flat world
in a dark forest found his face
some trace of the moon in
a darkened pool   rose
having drunk & bathed
to find the nameless ones around him

& the nameless ones entered him
somewhere beyond words

& the old gods abandoned him
in the mountains beyond his world

**

reach out to touch the pool's rim
i drank from fearfully

lay down beside & turned from
into a darker pool
                  within

no hope for my spells

how to taste what the tongue hates

Nūn
   where
Apophis dwells

aboard some boat
to ship oars
listening for
your breath

to seek the cup
finding it again & again

snake breath on your body

i have swallowed the sun

who swallows me
swallows the darkness

the lady dead

gone beyond prayer
beyond invocation

& you
who could not bring her to me
gone

to travel back
knowing i cannot drink of that cup again

the dark liquid that called Apophis forth
to be put away

                that taste on my tongue
old songs warn of

bitter
& warm

a taste that brings forth memory
a long way from the end of song

***

```
when i am not well
and shrieking
               (hiding my face
from my hands)
                    old gods
return
        to haunt me

i am screaming the end of their histories
knowing their mythologies shatter

my words swallow themselves
all that was grand & extravagant is lost in aimless gesturing
```

stasis

always
a season

bitter

to grow   beyond
complaint

who sits in
a room and
calls it city

who lives in
the past
         and says   present

all reference framed

.

open
the eyes

winter
thru a strange
window

how to
grow used to

a name

matins

i think i laid the cards out wrongly

read   backwards
as they fell

saw my past before me as my future
aged and gnarled voice of gallic ancestry
spectre of sonnets i could not understand

       dear lord

       father
       in all names

       i exhort thee

       king of wands

       show me
       my path

       what crowns me

"I see a serpent in Canada
 who courts me to his love"

          forgotten

Blake speaks to me of dreaming

i follow his spells into darker schemes

what is gained
from lingering
      in death's fingers?

the dreams you dream are portent to another world

distant

      and in a sphere of
its own

      "and round thy dark limbs on the Canadian
wilds I fold
feeble my spirit folds"

there is nothing to be gained
                    the bones in his
fingers crumble
the thot of him
        explodes

***

took me
to the store

laid me in
choc-o-late
          & more

wandered the streets
saw only her face
who is a dark omen
from another place

returned to my room
to lie-a-bed
dark choc'late thots
in my choc-o-late head

<u>photograph</u>

the single note
touches
the single man

pose
in singlet
& trousers

breathes "she
love me
        loves me
not"

the sun is in the wrong spot

holds the violin away

thinks "it is
too far
        to go
to reach
my heart
        (my soul)"

late night summer poem

one of those nights the chest aches with emptiness
which part of me missing?
                      what?

today i am writing these words

tomorrow i make them a poem

in lieu of a letter
i say what is least important
talk
     around the plain
truth

       it is fear
moves me to say these things

skirting the edge
i've skirted before
conscious always
i am not conscious of
the edge

        hello.

some strangers hands i make my own

with feeling

**

if the body fills out
it fills out with love

if it is empty
it is full of the loving of emptiness

always there are spaces

230

always there are places we go to feeling certain
things
lovingly finger familiar sorrows
& cling

**

sorrow's a luxury
you fill up with poems

love you have little of
& use more sparingly

none of which is true

when you love others you love them with words &
fingers
enter to give them those things you can

& when you have such nothing
you love only yourself
you fill your poems with self-love & loathing
& it is not poetry
                    it is dead

**

the poem begins & ends nowhere
being part of the flow you live with
starts when you're born
stepping in & out of
such moments you are aware
emerge as pages put in a book & titled
living always on the edges of
you are drawn into & cannot encompass
the flow of which is poetry

<u>circus days</u>

gathering
of years

still photos of

        my mother

1930
circus billboard

it was
the greatest show on earth

the greatest show
ever to hit
Plunkett, Saskatchewan

**

remember
as a kid

Casey Brothers
coming to town

hated all that
candy floss

        the rides were
lousey

once around this fucking little track
and that was the roller coaster

we must've spent three dollars there
perverts trying to buy us off with candy floss

i remember
Shaunna Sawin didn't go
coz
      they had such a
lousey show

**

lying on the each at
Port Dover

            they had
a permanent   arcade

dropped my quarter in
to watch the women
take off
            their clothes &
wrote a poem

            Beach at Port Dover

&
      after that
there was this
sudden storm

postcard between

for margaret avison

looked up & saw
the winter sun

                    clouds
half covering it

somewhere near
washington street
it came

into my ear
this morning

            again

a woman or
the sea
moved over me

like the clouds
till

        no focus

grown used to
by degrees

            and i thot

                "i have done with it"

vague

      like the clouds
      my language was

sun
disappearing from view

this poem for you

green lady grocer early morning song

early morning
raining

blues
        for a
green   lady

walk out the door

turned to snow

baby baby
i ain't got
no more
        to give you

no moon in
the sky

i don't know why
no no

goodbye green lady
i got to
go

**

you
cast your tent in
my midst

            just
too much flesh for
the skin to
bear

hyper-aware of every motion

goodbye baby
i'm heading cross an ocean
to an eastern shore

it's been a
long and a
losing
war

**

got up and
raised my head i'd
left it on
the bed

threw it out
the window but
it didn't
grow wings

one of those
things baby just
one of those
things

<u>uneven song</u>

i think i'm going mad

ain't no good times
to be had

press yr eyes
against the glass

the stars go past
& on
      into
nothingness

the rest is writ
ten the race is run

only the bad lines done

BIBLIOGRAPHIC NOTES

AE = As Elected: Selected Writing.
Vancouver: Talonbooks, 1980.

AG = The Alphabet Game: a bpNichol Reader.
Toronto: Coach House, 2007.

HH = An H in the Heart: bpNichol A Reader.
Toronto: McClelland and Stewart, 1994.

W = W)here?: The Other Canadian Poetry.
Erin, Ont: Press Porcepic, 1974.

Corrections made to the copy texts indicated, with
the original spelling appearing after the square bracket.

CYCLES ETC.

Original publication: Cleveland: 7 Flowers Press, 1965 [Ohio City Series 4]. Letter press cover with mimeo interior. 100 copies. "Cycle #25," "Bouquet for Dace," "Cycle #26," and "Politics #2" appear on green coloured paper, while "Glyph #2" and "Historical Implications of Turnips" are printed on grey paper.

"Bouquet for Dace" also appears in *Konfessions of an Elizabethan Fan Dancer* (London: Writers Forum, 1967) and in *Still Water* (Vancouver: Talonbooks, 1970).

"Historical Implications of Turnips" also appears in *Konfessions of an Elizabethan Fan Dancer* (London: Writers Forum, 1967), *JOURNEYING & the returns* (Toronto: Coach House, 1967), and *HH* as "turnips are" (135). A sound recording appears on *Motherlove* (Allied, 1968).

The images in this edition are taken from scans of a copy housed in the bpNichol archives at Special Collections and Rare Books, W.A.C. Bennett Library, Simon Fraser University. Thanks to Tony Power.

Converted to black and white images and clarified by Sharon Harris.

EYES

First publication in *An Anthology of Concrete Poetry*, edited by Emmett Williams (New York: Something Else, 1967).

Three images from the series also appear in *20th Century Poetry and Poetics*, 2nd Edition, edited by Gary Geddes (Toronto: Oxford UP, 1973).

In the Williams anthology, Nichol provides the following note on the sequence:

tight imagistic things. intended for what they teach the eye on one looking tho some tend to be pleasing if looked at a few times. executed as a unit which has become my standard concrete composing form. seldom singly. not meant as pictures but as syllabic and sub-syllabic messages for who care to listen ... i chose this unit EYES, which not too coincidently is the most recent, as the best things i've done ... with CONCRETE i tend to think of only the most recent things as mine. all the rest go into a literary LIMBO.

The images in this edition were scanned from the Williams anthology, and enlarged and clarified by Sharon Harris.

JOURNEYING & THE RETURNS

First published as part of the *JOURNEYING & the returns* boxed collection (Toronto: Coach House, 1967). Cover photo by Andy Phillips.

The poem is printed on grey paper in various coloured inks: "Blues on Green" (blue-green); "Fire and Water" (yellow); "Ancient Maps of the Real World" (dark green); "Beginning. And. End" (cyan); "Letters from a Rainy Season" (dark blue).

Sections from this sequence appear in *AE* (69–70), *AG* (130–142), *HH* (112–120), *New Wave Canada* (ed. Raymond Souster. Toronto: Contact, 1966: 132), *Canadian Poetry Vol. 2* (eds. Jack David and Robert Lecker. Toronto: General, 1982: 263–264), and *The Last Blewointment Anthology Vol. 2* (ed. bill bissett. Toronto: Nightwood, 1986: 38).

Inside flaps of the book, excluding a biographic note on Nichol, read:

> The person moves thru the world and is moved by the need to communicate. It is not surprising that in his first book of non-concrete poetry the concerns of bpNichol centre around communication and the presence of or lack of it in relationships.
> […]
> This book arose of physical and mental journeys in and between Vancouver, Winnipeg and Toronto. It is the quiet side that 'New Wave Canada' hinted at—a man writing out of periods of intense pain and change in his life. It is not the side that Ganglia has shown but rather the side that his friend David Phillips spoke of in a poem written to him
>> 'old enough to have
>> old friends
>>
>> no longer
>> wonderful out of
>> necessity'

The book's colophon reads:

> *parts of* JOURNEYING & the returns *appeared in* Blew Ointment *and* New Wave Canada.
>
> this poem is also dedicated to:
>
> James Alexander
> Bill Bissett

Barb Nyberg
David Phillips
Dace Puce

thanx to Margaret Avison, Dave Aylward and particularly Wayne Clifford – all of whom offered encouragement and criticism

The *J&R* box also contains a reproduction of letter from Margaret Avison, relating to *J&R*:

> *Dear bpn*
> *The range of simple terms finds a sure place in language*
> *– salt water and tap water, beach fire and astronomical*
> *fire and living energy, space framed and leaking and*
> *hollowing and flowing down transcontinental RRtracks,*
> *lives finding singular form in an infolding and opening-*
> *out whole.*
>
> *Can there be mime in words? – your poem comes to*
> *that: magnetic flow of force; speaking that does not*
> *distance a person who hears; giving and never giving*
> *anything away.*
>
> *I like a cup, cupped hands – (& other sequences like*
> *that, with other terms). The ocean-wash under the on-*
> *flowing of the poem is exciting – e.g. the part where the*
> *poignantly present is found, on a round earth, with the*
> *journey falling away eastward and the westcoast's leaves*
> *falling oceanwards, out of time – and right after that,*
> *the poem of Canadian absence "against the west wall*
> *called ocean," all a depressed placeless place. "Is" and "is*

246

not" come clear, which I found heartening indeed.
thanks.

Margaret

This version transcribed from a copy of the book housed at the Clara Thomas Archives and Special Collections, York University.

RUTH

First publication: Toronto: Fleye Press, 1967 [Luv 5]. Reprinted with manuscript facsimile and introduction by David UU (Hamilton, Ont: Mindware, 1993 [The Berkeley Horse 43]).

The sequence also appears in *HH* (44–47).

This version transcribed from the 1967 edition, and checked against the 1993 reprint.

THE YEAR OF THE FROG

Original publication: Toronto: Ganglia, 1967 [Ganglia Concrete Series 3]. Printed with green ink on cream paper.

A page from this sequence appears in *W* (44).

Title page indicates that these images are "a study of the Frog from SCRAPTURES: ninth sequence". "Scraptures: 9th Sequence" appeared in *GrOnk* 1.2 (1967) and is currently found in *The Martyrology Book(s) 7 &* (Toronto: Coach House, 1990).

Scanned by Sharon Harris.

BALLADS OF THE RESTLESS ARE

Original publication: Sacramento: Runcible Spoon, 1968.
Second "corrected" Edition: Ottawa: CURVD H&Z, 2006.
[Afterword by William Cool].
   A selection from the sequence also appears in *W* (42).
   A recording of Nichol's reading of the piece can be found
on the *Ear Rational* audiocassette (Milwaukee: New Fire
Tapes/Membrane P, 1982).
   The poem begins with an introductory note by Phillip
Workman [pseud. bpNichol] which reads:

> I first published this piece as part of
> the "Black Ribbon" series in 1962 along
> with books like Dave Aylward's "A History
> of Nothing" (which I understand Ganglia
> Press is reissuing) and my own "Annotated
> Chance."
> Since this piece was written so much has
> happened that parts of it may seem archaic
> (part of the charm perhaps) but its impor-
> tance and relevance remains, particularly
> in the list of current research into lan-
> guage sources. Read it and speak it and
> get back to your own.

The sequence also concludes with a note:

> further verses and other versions exist.
> For a more complete listing consult
> bpNichol's unpublished ANNOTAOTED
> TEXTS or THE LETTER R: a compleat

history – a destroyed text by dave
aylward. Also relevant THE HISTORY OF
NOTHING by Phillip Workman, published
by Black Ribbon Press, Vancouver, 1963.

This version transcribed from a copy of 1968 edition held in
the Thomas Fisher Rare Book Library, and checked against
the 2006 edition.

Version One, Section 10, last line: mo t o] mo r o

KON 66 & 67

Original publication: Toronto: Ganglia, 1968 [*Gronk* 2.1].
Reprinted, Ottawa: above/ground, 2002.
    This version scanned by Sharon Harris from the 2002
reprint.

LAMENT

Original publication: Toronto: Ganglia, 1969.
    Colophon page reads: "this poem was first performed
as part of a reading in conjunction with the opening of an
exhibition of concrete poetry at UBC gallery of fine arts. /
april 1969"
    Variant from series appears in *AE* (57) and *HH* (38).
    A recording of Nichol reading *Lament* is featured in
Michael Ondaatje's documentary film *Sons of Captain Poetry*
(1970) and in Brian Nash's film *bp: pushing the boundaries*
(1997).
    Scanned by Sharon Harris.

BEACH HEAD

Original publication: Sacramento: Runcible Spoon, 1970.
Cover art by D.r. wagner.
Nichol includes this final note regarding the poem's genealogy:

> D.r. sent these back to me & said could i make any
> (questions) changes to these i wanted to and send
> them back. i couldn't. i made only one poem differnet
> [sic] & left it up to him. i am no longer the person i
> was when i wrote these. my musculature is different &
> (as a result) my breath. breath lines that made sense
> then no longer make sense. the LAND section (one
> long poem) has the panicky short breath line i was in
> at the time, that poem written in a period of time that
> terror ruled me as never before or since. if i changed
> it now it would make no sense. what could be more
> illogical than to look back & say that the breath line
> makes no sense when in fact that was how i breathed
> then? these poems are offered up in friendship to
> whoever hears them and breaths them with their own
> body.

echoes] echos
receded] receeded
ourselves] oursleves
memory] momory

THE OTHER SIDE OF THE ROOM

Original publication: Toronto: Weed/flower, 1971. Cover art

by Barbara Caruso.

"after hokusai" appears in *AE* (60)

"the other side of the room" appears in *AE* (68).

"circus days" appears in *AG* (143–144) & *HH* (55–56)

"seaquence" appears in *HH* (52–54)

"stasis" appears in *AG* (145).

"this morning the dream will not visit me" appears in *HH* (51)

"late night summer poem" appears in *Canadian Poetry Vol. 2* (Toronto: General, 1982: 270–271)

"took me" published as the pamphlet *The Chocolate Poem* (Toronto: Ganglia, 1966).

Transcribed from a copy held in the Scott Library, York University.

BIO/BIBLIOGRAPHIC

In preparing *bp: beginnings*, beyond the secondary texts directly cited in my introduction, I also consulted numerous Nichol-related materials regarding dates and events. Most valuable was Nelson Ball's edited edition of *Konfessions of Elizabethan Fan Dancer* (Toronto: Coach House, 2004), which is a model of design, organization, and careful research, especially the concluding bibliography of Nichol's early periodical appearances. I also frequently referred to the festschrift for Nichol published as *Open Letter 6.5/6* in 1986 (particularly jwcurry's "Notes toward a beepliography"), Frank Davey's biography *aka bpNichol* (Toronto: ECW, 2012), and Jack David's introduction to Nichol's selected writing *As Elected* (Vancouver: Talonbooks, 1980).

COLOPHON

Manufactured as the first edition of
bp: beginnings in the spring
of 2014 by BookThug.

Distributed in Canada by the
Literary Press Group: www.lpg.ca

Distributed in the USA by
Small Press Distribution: www.spdbooks.org

Shop online at www.bookthug.ca

BOOK
PRODUCTION
WAR ECONOMY
STANDARD

Type + design by Jay MillAr
Copy edited by Ruth Zuchter